D0833498

ILLUMINATED

SCRIPTURE JOURNAL

ENGLISH STANDARD VERSION

EPHESIANS

CROSSWAY

WHEATON, ILLINOIS — ESV.ORG

ESV® Illuminated Scripture Journal: Ephesians

The Holy Bible, English Standard Version® (ESV®)
Copyright © 2001 by Crossway,
a publishing ministry of Good News Publishers.
All rights reserved.

ESV® Text Edition: 2016

Printed in China
Published by Crossway
Wheaton, Illinois 60187, U.S.A.
crossway.org

Crossway is a not-for-profit publishing ministry that exists solely for the purpose of publishing the Good News of the Gospel and the Truth of God's Word, the Bible. A portion of the purchase price of every ESV Bible is donated to help support Bible distribution ministry around the world.

The ESV Bible is free online and on mobile devices everywhere worldwide, including a selection of free Bible resources, at esv.org.

RRDS	28	27	26	25	24	23	22	21
19	18	17	16	15	14	13	12	11

PREFACE

The Bible

The words of the Bible are the very words of God our Creator speaking to us. They are completely truthful;[1] they are pure;[2] they are powerful;[3] and they are wise and righteous.[4] We should read these words with reverence and awe,[5] and with joy and delight.[6] Through these words God gives us eternal life,[7] and daily nourishes our spiritual lives.[8]

The ESV Translation

The English Standard Version® (ESV®) stands in the classic stream of English Bible translations that goes back nearly five centuries. In this stream, accurate faithfulness to the original text is combined with simplicity, beauty, and dignity of expression. Our goal has been to carry forward this legacy for this generation and generations to come.

The ESV is an "essentially literal" translation that seeks as far as possible to reproduce the meaning and structure of the original text and the personal style of each Bible writer. We have sought to be "as literal as possible" while maintaining clear expression and literary excellence. Therefore the ESV is well suited for both personal reading and church ministry, for devotional reflection and serious study, and for Scripture memorization.

---

[1] Ps. 119:160; Prov. 30:5; Titus 1:2; Heb. 6:18 [2] Ps. 12:6 [3] Jer. 23:29; Heb. 4:12; 1 Pet. 1:23
[4] Ps. 19:7–11 [5] Deut. 28:58; Ps. 119:74; Isa. 66:2 [6] Ps. 19:7–11; 119:14, 97, 103; Jer. 15:16
[7] John 6:68; 1 Pet. 1:23 [8] Deut. 32:46; Matt. 4:4

The ESV Publishing Team

The ESV publishing team has included more than a hundred people. The fourteen-member Translation Oversight Committee benefited from the work of fifty biblical experts serving as Translation Review Scholars and from the comments of the more than fifty members of the Advisory Council. This international team from many denominations shares a common commitment to the truth of God's Word and to historic Christian orthodoxy.

To God's Honor and Praise

We know that no Bible translation is perfect; but we also know that God uses imperfect and inadequate things to his honor and praise. So to God the Father, Son, and Holy Spirit—and to his people—we offer what we have done, with our prayers that it may prove useful, with gratitude for much help given, and with ongoing wonder that our God should ever have entrusted to us so momentous a task.

To God alone be the glory!
The Translation Oversight Committee

THE LETTER OF PAUL TO THE

EPHESIANS

Greeting

1 Paul, an apostle of Christ Jesus by the will of God,
To the saints who are in Ephesus, and are faithful in Christ
Jesus:

²Grace to you and peace from God our Father and the Lord
Jesus Christ.

Spiritual Blessings in Christ

³Blessed be the God and Father of our Lord Jesus Christ, who
has blessed us in Christ with every spiritual blessing in the heavenly places, ⁴even as he chose us in him before the foundation of
the world, that we should be holy and blameless before him. In
love ⁵he predestined us for adoption to himself as sons through
Jesus Christ, according to the purpose of his will, ⁶to the praise
of his glorious grace, with which he has blessed us in the Beloved.
⁷In him we have redemption through his blood, the forgiveness
of our trespasses, according to the riches of his grace, ⁸which he
lavished upon us, in all wisdom and insight ⁹making known to
us the mystery of his will, according to his purpose, which he
set forth in Christ ¹⁰as a plan for the fullness of time, to unite all
things in him, things in heaven and things on earth.

¹¹In him we have obtained an inheritance, having been predestined according to the purpose of him who works all things

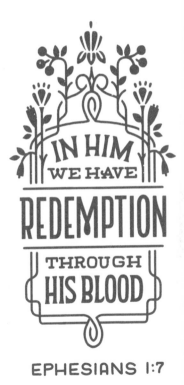

IN HIM
WE HAVE
REDEMPTION
THROUGH
HIS BLOOD

EPHESIANS 1:7

according to the counsel of his will, [12] so that we who were the first to hope in Christ might be to the praise of his glory. [13] In him you also, when you heard the word of truth, the gospel of your salvation, and believed in him, were sealed with the promised Holy Spirit, [14] who is the guarantee of our inheritance until we acquire possession of it, to the praise of his glory.

Thanksgiving and Prayer

[15] For this reason, because I have heard of your faith in the Lord Jesus and your love toward all the saints, [16] I do not cease to give thanks for you, remembering you in my prayers, [17] that the God of our Lord Jesus Christ, the Father of glory, may give you the Spirit of wisdom and of revelation in the knowledge of him, [18] having the eyes of your hearts enlightened, that you may know what is the hope to which he has called you, what are the riches of his glorious inheritance in the saints, [19] and what is the immeasurable greatness of his power toward us who believe, according to the working of his great might [20] that he worked in Christ when he raised him from the dead and seated him at his right hand in the heavenly places, [21] far above all rule and authority and power and dominion, and above every name that is named, not only in this age but also in the one to come. [22] And he put all things under his feet and gave him as head over all things to the church, [23] which is his body, the fullness of him who fills all in all.

By Grace Through Faith

2 And you were dead in the trespasses and sins [2] in which you once walked, following the course of this world, following the prince of the power of the air, the spirit that is now at work

in the sons of disobedience— **3** among whom we all once lived in the passions of our flesh, carrying out the desires of the body and the mind, and were by nature children of wrath, like the rest of mankind. **4** But God, being rich in mercy, because of the great love with which he loved us, **5** even when we were dead in our trespasses, made us alive together with Christ—by grace you have been saved— **6** and raised us up with him and seated us with him in the heavenly places in Christ Jesus, **7** so that in the coming ages he might show the immeasurable riches of his grace in kindness toward us in Christ Jesus. **8** For by grace you have been saved through faith. And this is not your own doing; it is the gift of God, **9** not a result of works, so that no one may boast. **10** For we are his workmanship, created in Christ Jesus for good works, which God prepared beforehand, that we should walk in them.

One in Christ

11 Therefore remember that at one time you Gentiles in the flesh, called "the uncircumcision" by what is called the circumcision, which is made in the flesh by hands— **12** remember that you were at that time separated from Christ, alienated from the commonwealth of Israel and strangers to the covenants of promise, having no hope and without God in the world. **13** But now in Christ Jesus you who once were far off have been brought near by the blood of Christ. **14** For he himself is our peace, who has made us both one and has broken down in his flesh the dividing wall of hostility **15** by abolishing the law of commandments expressed in ordinances, that he might create in himself one new man in place of the two, so making peace, **16** and might reconcile us both to God in one body through the

cross, thereby killing the hostility. [17] And he came and preached peace to you who were far off and peace to those who were near. [18] For through him we both have access in one Spirit to the Father. [19] So then you are no longer strangers and aliens, but you are fellow citizens with the saints and members of the household of God, [20] built on the foundation of the apostles and prophets, Christ Jesus himself being the cornerstone, [21] in whom the whole structure, being joined together, grows into a holy temple in the Lord. [22] In him you also are being built together into a dwelling place for God by the Spirit.

The Mystery of the Gospel Revealed

3 For this reason I, Paul, a prisoner of Christ Jesus on behalf of you Gentiles— [2] assuming that you have heard of the stewardship of God's grace that was given to me for you, [3] how the mystery was made known to me by revelation, as I have written briefly. [4] When you read this, you can perceive my insight into the mystery of Christ, [5] which was not made known to the sons of men in other generations as it has now been revealed to his holy apostles and prophets by the Spirit. [6] This mystery is that the Gentiles are fellow heirs, members of the same body, and partakers of the promise in Christ Jesus through the gospel.

[7] Of this gospel I was made a minister according to the gift of God's grace, which was given me by the working of his power. [8] To me, though I am the very least of all the saints, this grace was given, to preach to the Gentiles the unsearchable riches of Christ, [9] and to bring to light for everyone what is the plan of the mystery hidden for ages in God, who created all things, [10] so that through the church the manifold wisdom of God might now be made known to the rulers and authorities

in the heavenly places. ¹¹ This was according to the eternal purpose that he has realized in Christ Jesus our Lord, ¹² in whom we have boldness and access with confidence through our faith in him. ¹³ So I ask you not to lose heart over what I am suffering for you, which is your glory.

Prayer for Spiritual Strength

¹⁴ For this reason I bow my knees before the Father, ¹⁵ from whom every family in heaven and on earth is named, ¹⁶ that according to the riches of his glory he may grant you to be strengthened with power through his Spirit in your inner being, ¹⁷ so that Christ may dwell in your hearts through faith—that you, being rooted and grounded in love, ¹⁸ may have strength to comprehend with all the saints what is the breadth and length and height and depth, ¹⁹ and to know the love of Christ that surpasses knowledge, that you may be filled with all the fullness of God.

²⁰ Now to him who is able to do far more abundantly than all that we ask or think, according to the power at work within us, ²¹ to him be glory in the church and in Christ Jesus throughout all generations, forever and ever. Amen.

Unity in the Body of Christ

4 I therefore, a prisoner for the Lord, urge you to walk in a manner worthy of the calling to which you have been called, ² with all humility and gentleness, with patience, bearing with one another in love, ³ eager to maintain the unity of the Spirit in the bond of peace. ⁴ There is one body and one Spirit—just as you were called to the one hope that belongs to your call— ⁵ one Lord, one faith, one baptism, ⁶ one God and

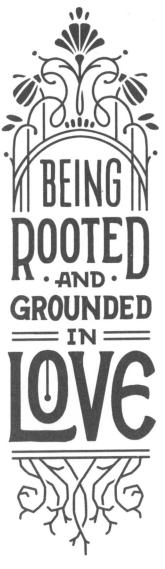

BEING ROOTED ·AND· GROUNDED IN LOVE

EPHESIANS 3:17

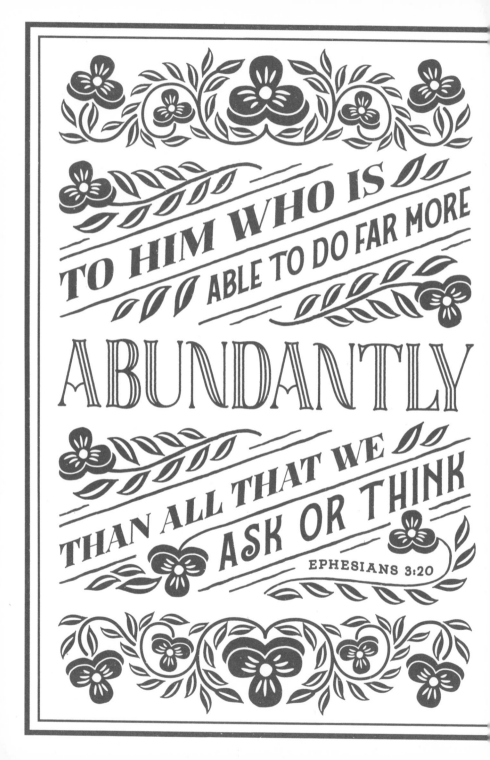

Father of all, who is over all and through all and in all. ⁷But grace was given to each one of us according to the measure of Christ's gift. ⁸Therefore it says,

> "When he ascended on high he led a host of
> captives,
>   and he gave gifts to men."

⁹(In saying, "He ascended," what does it mean but that he had also descended into the lower regions, the earth? ¹⁰He who descended is the one who also ascended far above all the heavens, that he might fill all things.) ¹¹And he gave the apostles, the prophets, the evangelists, the shepherds and teachers, ¹²to equip the saints for the work of ministry, for building up the body of Christ, ¹³until we all attain to the unity of the faith and of the knowledge of the Son of God, to mature manhood, to the measure of the stature of the fullness of Christ, ¹⁴so that we may no longer be children, tossed to and fro by the waves and carried about by every wind of doctrine, by human cunning, by craftiness in deceitful schemes. ¹⁵Rather, speaking the truth in love, we are to grow up in every way into him who is the head, into Christ, ¹⁶from whom the whole body, joined and held together by every joint with which it is equipped, when each part is working properly, makes the body grow so that it builds itself up in love.

The New Life

¹⁷Now this I say and testify in the Lord, that you must no longer walk as the Gentiles do, in the futility of their minds. ¹⁸They are darkened in their understanding, alienated from

the life of God because of the ignorance that is in them, due to their hardness of heart. [19] They have become callous and have given themselves up to sensuality, greedy to practice every kind of impurity. [20] But that is not the way you learned Christ!— [21] assuming that you have heard about him and were taught in him, as the truth is in Jesus, [22] to put off your old self, which belongs to your former manner of life and is corrupt through deceitful desires, [23] and to be renewed in the spirit of your minds, [24] and to put on the new self, created after the likeness of God in true righteousness and holiness.

[25] Therefore, having put away falsehood, let each one of you speak the truth with his neighbor, for we are members one of another. [26] Be angry and do not sin; do not let the sun go down on your anger, [27] and give no opportunity to the devil. [28] Let the thief no longer steal, but rather let him labor, doing honest work with his own hands, so that he may have something to share with anyone in need. [29] Let no corrupting talk come out of your mouths, but only such as is good for building up, as fits the occasion, that it may give grace to those who hear. [30] And do not grieve the Holy Spirit of God, by whom you were sealed for the day of redemption. [31] Let all bitterness and wrath and anger and clamor and slander be put away from you, along with all malice. [32] Be kind to one another, tenderhearted, forgiving one another, as God in Christ forgave you.

Walk in Love

5 Therefore be imitators of God, as beloved children. [2] And walk in love, as Christ loved us and gave himself up for us, a fragrant offering and sacrifice to God.

THEREFORE
BE
IMITATORS
OF
GOD

EPHESIANS 5:1

[3] But sexual immorality and all impurity or covetousness must not even be named among you, as is proper among saints. [4] Let there be no filthiness nor foolish talk nor crude joking, which are out of place, but instead let there be thanksgiving. [5] For you may be sure of this, that everyone who is sexually immoral or impure, or who is covetous (that is, an idolater), has no inheritance in the kingdom of Christ and God. [6] Let no one deceive you with empty words, for because of these things the wrath of God comes upon the sons of disobedience. [7] Therefore do not become partners with them; [8] for at one time you were darkness, but now you are light in the Lord. Walk as children of light [9] (for the fruit of light is found in all that is good and right and true), [10] and try to discern what is pleasing to the Lord. [11] Take no part in the unfruitful works of darkness, but instead expose them. [12] For it is shameful even to speak of the things that they do in secret. [13] But when anything is exposed by the light, it becomes visible, [14] for anything that becomes visible is light. Therefore it says,

> "Awake, O sleeper,
>   and arise from the dead,
>   and Christ will shine on you."

[15] Look carefully then how you walk, not as unwise but as wise, [16] making the best use of the time, because the days are evil. [17] Therefore do not be foolish, but understand what the will of the Lord is. [18] And do not get drunk with wine, for that is debauchery, but be filled with the Spirit, [19] addressing one another in psalms and hymns and spiritual songs, singing and making melody to the Lord with your heart, [20] giving thanks

always and for everything to God the Father in the name of our Lord Jesus Christ, ²¹ submitting to one another out of reverence for Christ.

Wives and Husbands

²² Wives, submit to your own husbands, as to the Lord. ²³ For the husband is the head of the wife even as Christ is the head of the church, his body, and is himself its Savior. ²⁴ Now as the church submits to Christ, so also wives should submit in everything to their husbands.

²⁵ Husbands, love your wives, as Christ loved the church and gave himself up for her, ²⁶ that he might sanctify her, having cleansed her by the washing of water with the word, ²⁷ so that he might present the church to himself in splendor, without spot or wrinkle or any such thing, that she might be holy and without blemish. ²⁸ In the same way husbands should love their wives as their own bodies. He who loves his wife loves himself. ²⁹ For no one ever hated his own flesh, but nourishes and cherishes it, just as Christ does the church, ³⁰ because we are members of his body. ³¹ "Therefore a man shall leave his father and mother and hold fast to his wife, and the two shall become one flesh." ³² This mystery is profound, and I am saying that it refers to Christ and the church. ³³ However, let each one of you love his wife as himself, and let the wife see that she respects her husband.

Children and Parents

6 Children, obey your parents in the Lord, for this is right. ² "Honor your father and mother" (this is the first commandment with a promise), ³ "that it may go well with you and that you may live long in the land." ⁴ Fathers, do not provoke

your children to anger, but bring them up in the discipline and instruction of the Lord.

Bondservants and Masters

5 Bondservants, obey your earthly masters with fear and trembling, with a sincere heart, as you would Christ, 6 not by the way of eye-service, as people-pleasers, but as bondservants of Christ, doing the will of God from the heart, 7 rendering service with a good will as to the Lord and not to man, 8 knowing that whatever good anyone does, this he will receive back from the Lord, whether he is a bondservant or is free. 9 Masters, do the same to them, and stop your threatening, knowing that he who is both their Master and yours is in heaven, and that there is no partiality with him.

The Whole Armor of God

10 Finally, be strong in the Lord and in the strength of his might. 11 Put on the whole armor of God, that you may be able to stand against the schemes of the devil. 12 For we do not wrestle against flesh and blood, but against the rulers, against the authorities, against the cosmic powers over this present darkness, against the spiritual forces of evil in the heavenly places. 13 Therefore take up the whole armor of God, that you may be able to withstand in the evil day, and having done all, to stand firm. 14 Stand therefore, having fastened on the belt of truth, and having put on the breastplate of righteousness, 15 and, as shoes for your feet, having put on the readiness given by the gospel of peace. 16 In all circumstances take up the shield of faith, with which you can extinguish all the flaming darts of the evil one; 17 and take the helmet of salvation, and the sword

PUT ON the WHOLE Armor OF God

EPHESIANS 6:11

of the Spirit, which is the word of God, [18] praying at all times in the Spirit, with all prayer and supplication. To that end, keep alert with all perseverance, making supplication for all the saints, [19] and also for me, that words may be given to me in opening my mouth boldly to proclaim the mystery of the gospel, [20] for which I am an ambassador in chains, that I may declare it boldly, as I ought to speak.

Final Greetings

[21] So that you also may know how I am and what I am doing, Tychicus the beloved brother and faithful minister in the Lord will tell you everything. [22] I have sent him to you for this very purpose, that you may know how we are, and that he may encourage your hearts.

[23] Peace be to the brothers, and love with faith, from God the Father and the Lord Jesus Christ. [24] Grace be with all who love our Lord Jesus Christ with love incorruptible.